FAMOUS TIMES

HISTORIC WOOLSHEDS OF HAWKES BAY

AN ARCHITECTURAL PILGRIMAGE.
Woolsheds over 100 years old.

ANGUS GORDON

Copyright © 2019 by Angus Gordon
All rights reserved. No part of this book may be reproduced, scanned,
or distributed in any printed or electronic form without permission.
First Edition: January 2019
Printed in the United States of America
ISBN: 1642540781
ISBN: 9781642540789

I wish to acknowledge and thank the following:

All the woolshed owners who let me photograph their sheds and gave me information on the history of those sheds;

Miriam MacGregor, whose book ' Early Stations of Hawkes Bay,' has been invaluable to me for the early history of a lot of the stations;

Michael and Carola Hudson of Gwavas, and Tom and Joanna Lowry of Okawa, who let me photograph their historic old photos of the shearing gangs;

And I wish to apologise in advance if I have missed out any woolsheds that might have qualified as over 100 years old. I have had to eliminate may fine woolsheds as they didn't fit that category, but I might also have inadvertently just not known about some.

INTRODUCTION

The idea for this book came to me purely by accident. In 2007 I was approached by a reporter from HB Today who wanted to write an article on myself and my book 'In the Shadow of the Cape,' which I had written in 2004. I said I was reluctant to do another story as I had already had wide publicity over the slip that devastated the hill behind our house in July 2006. The reporter was very persistent, as they can be, and so I said I'd only agree if we found a new angle to the story. I was standing outside our own woolshed at the time, talking to Ian Richardson, my partner in a new business doing farm shows for tourists that we had started in the old shed in 2006. 'I know,' I said to the reporter. 'I'm wanting to do a book on the historic sheds of Hawkes Bay, so we can use that as the storyline.' This was actually the first time I knew anything about such a scheme, but he agreed, and so I was committed.

I have since travelled thousands of kilometres. I did 1500 kms in my Holden Ute in just three days in the first week of May 2010, driving up every road off Highway 50 to the bottom of the Ruahine Ranges, driving in to Putere and then around the Cricklewood Road, travelling to Weber and then back up the coast, doing what I love best, noseying around a part of the world which goes mostly un-noticed these days, but which, as far as I am concerned, is one of the most beautiful places in the world, with a benevolent climate as an added bonus.

The Hawkes Bay pastoral farming industry was once synonymous with wealth. There was no insult worse that a radical student at Victoria University could throw at you in the 60's than that you were nothing ' but a wealthy Hawkes Bay Farmer's son.' I, who had pretensions to being a slight radical myself, by wanting to be a writer and a poet, was loth to admit to my fellow marchers as we processed through the streets of Wellington on yet another protest march, that I had endured a very privileged upbringing in the heart of the enemy territory. Now, and Hawkes Bay is famous for its wine, food, weather, and fruit, leaving the pastoral industry in the dismal position of being rather sidelined, considered a sort of sunset industry, with the 'lifestyle' factor sometimes being the only justification for farmers to cling onto their grossly over-valued properties with minimal cash flow.

I was brought up during the Korean Wool Boom years. In fact I was born in the very year, 1950, when the Korean War began. The next twenty years were ones of great prosperity for farmers. Even farmers on marginal dry land on 500 acres (the standard ballot block size for returned soldiers after the 2nd World War) could make a good living out of the big three: wool, lamb meat and beef. Most of those 500 acre farms have now either been bought and added onto bigger properties or broken up into lifestyle blocks if they are within the 20 minute range of Hastings, Havelock North or Napier.

That is not to say that all is gloom and doom. A drive down the coast properties, starting from Clifton, and covering the other three intact stations that were part of Clifton; Cape Kidnappers, Haupouri and Taurapa, ducking in at Waimarama and Cabbage Tree Flat, poking into Te Apiti, driving past Waipari (ex Mangakuri shed) Rangitapu, Whenouahou, Te Manuiri, and stopping at Blackhead before travelling on down the coast to the monster Porangahau woolshed, then arriving at one of the jewels of the coast, Tautane, 9000 acres of prime breeding country, passing the lovely Burnview complex before climbing the windswept coastal hills of Akitio and finishing at the graceful shed at Moanaroa, will reveal a wealth of continuing history in the making.

When I was doing the final coast run as I called it, down to Akitio, I took my son Tom, the sixth generation of our family to have lived at Clifton, and an English friend of his, Tony, with me. We stopped at the Herbertville camping ground for the night and ended up having a delicious meal in the Herbertville pub. It was full of rowdy young shepherds from around the area, mainly Tautane, a property that my mother's family, the Herricks, have been involved in for over 100 years. After dinner I went to bed across the way, but Tom and Tony stayed on. They eventually struggled to bed in the wee hours. Tom looked the worst for wear in the morning, with scratches all over his arms and legs and when I asked him what had happened he related to me how he had got involved in an old custom for new shepherds at Tautane. They, and he, had clambered up onto the Steel beam that ran across the room, and had then had to fit themselves through the triangular support bars that reinforced the beam. Needless to say one couldn't be carrying any surplus fat, which is why Tony explained how he was unable to participate.

I set a criteria for this book that the sheds must be over 100 years old, which luckily included the first decade of the 1900's, because it was during this time that many of the huge early estates were being broken up by the Seddon Government and new properties being established, with of course new woolsheds. A classic example of this is the stunning Olrig shed, built in 1907. Others include the Haupouri shed, built by my grandfather at Ocean Beach for his brother Edward in 1906, when that part of Clifton was cut off. After that time the sheds seem to lose their individuality and are mainly built of corrugated iron. Before that and every shed was different from the next, some even being architecturally designed, the main similarities being that they were mainly always made with weatherboard timber on the outside walls, with tongue in groove Matai or Rimu floorboards. Some of the very early sheds, like Gwavas and the Mission shed had wooden shingles on the roofs. These have now been covered over with corrugated iron. The majority of the early big sheds, most of which are still in immaculate order, were built to last, but have all been well looked after as well over the years. The Clifton shed was completely repiled with concrete piles by my father in the 1960's, because of the awkward levels created by the 1931 earthquake.

Some of the very early sheds, like Poporangi, Okawa, Mangatoro are unfortunately beyond repair, but still retain a charm of design, that make them very attractive buildings to look at. One of the oldest, and biggest, the fabulous Maraekakaho shed, so well built that it is still in very good repair, despite not being used to the extent that it was originally intended, is a prime example of all that was elegant, individual and well built in those original old sheds. Part of the reason for the immense size of the early sheds was that they were originally built for blade shearers. For example Clifton was originally a twenty stand blade shearing shed, reduced to a twelve stand shed when machines were introduced in 1904, and then further reduced to a 6 stand shed when one of the six stand shafts was transferred to Haupouri. There could be as many as 40 people involved with shearing in those days, including the shepherds. I have a picture outside the Clifton Woolshed taken in 1893, of about that number. We were fortunate for such a number when the original homestead was burned down in 1898 during shearing time. There was not enough water to save the house but all the antique Indian furniture inside the building was saved though by all the shearers and shepherds and is still in the present day homestead thanks to them.

Many of the properties included here are defined by the woolsheds. They give the property its focal point. Of course there are many exceptions to this, where the old homesteads define the property, the most notable of these being, Akitio, Aramoana, Clifton, Tunanui, Matapiro, Okawa, Wallingford, Orua Wharo, Hinerangi, Gwavas, Ashcott, Forest gate, Springvale, and Whana Whana to name the most obvious. All the aforementioned homesteads, most of them well over 100 years old, are still all lived in, and are in immaculate condition. With the exception of Akitio, Matapiro and Orua Wharo, they are all lived in by descendants of the original settlers. So there is still a continuity in the pastoral history of the Bay, where most of these properties are now into the 5th, 6th, and 7th generation of the family to have lived, farmed and struggled to survive on their very special properties, especially in these increasingly difficult times we seem to be in with agriculture.

This book then is a sort architectural pilgrimage paying homage to the vision of our ancestors, but it is also a tribute to all those farmers who have lovingly maintained their old sheds, instead of demolishing them for a featureless modern shed.

Akitio

Technically in Northern Wairarapa, but because all it's business gravitates to Dannevirke and it's owners live in Havelock North, I have included it here, along with the Moanaroa shed. These are two of the most imposing sheds to be seen anywhere in New Zealand. Akitio is currently farmed by the fifth generation of the same family, the Armstrongs, who originally purchased it in 1875. It is still 3600 hectares, and the current owners, Edwin and Jenny Kight, whose children are the 6th generation of the family to be at Akitio, live in Havelock North, having sold the two storeyed homestead. They are concentrating on planting a lot of the harder country in pines. They are active participants in the Emissions Trading Scheme. At the end of 2010 they had about 1300 hectares in trees, with more to come. The woolshed is still in magnificent order, and was one of three in the area that were architecturally designed and built in the 1880's, the other two being Moanaroa and Tautane. Like the other two, Akitio was originally built as a 16 stand blade shearing shed, with 8 stands down either side of the building. Now it has been completely reconfigured inside and has an 8 stand raised L-board in the centre of the shed.

Apley shearers quarters looking towards the Kaweka ranges.

Apley

Originally the outstation of Sir George Whitmore's enormous Rissington Station, this 15,000 acre property was sold in 1873 for the huge sum of 30,500 pounds to W.T.Buckland of Auckland. The next year he sold the whole block to J.N.Williams for 37,300 pounds. In 1879 Williams sold off Apley in three smaller blocks for 46,855 pounds. The 6000 acre Apley block went to William Nelson who then sold it to his son-in-law, Harold Russell from Sherenden. In 1906 Harold sold to the Bells but remained as the mortgagor. But when the Bells went bankrupt he took it back and resold to the Wright family, who also went bankrupt in 1929, forcing Russell to take the property back again. The Russells managed to sell off blocks until in 1963, when Chris Sherratt bought the 1000 acre homestead block, and 700 acres of the neighbours. In 2001, after various subdivisions, he sold the remaining 700 acres with the homestead to Graham Webb.

Aramoana

14000 acres was taken off Blackhead by Alexander McHardy in 1906, but the 8000 acre Motere block was sold the next year. With different sales and additions in 1917 the station then settled on 6000 acres until 1935, when the property was subdivided, with G.F.McHardy getting 2800 acres at Aramoana and D.G.McHardy getting 3300 acres at Ouepoto. Access to the property was usually along the beach at low tide between Blackhead and Pourerere until the road was finished in 1954. Hence the name Aramoana, which means sea path. The 8 stand shed was built in 1907 by the coast but was reduced to 6 stands with the reduction in the size of the farm. The shed is no longer in use as the land around it was sold for a beach development in the early 2000's, but it has been kept in immaculate condition by the owners of the development, the David Mossmans and the David Hansens. In 2011 there was a weatherbomb on this stretch of the coast from Cape Kidnappers to Porangahau delivering up to 800 millimetres in 36 hours. A massive slip from the hill behind smashed into the back of the shed, causing extensive damage along the back. The building was lovingly restored by the developers to its present condition. Aramoana Station, now approximately 1500 acres, is still owned by the McHardy family, and is run by Chip McHardy.

Aramoana, showing the restoration work at the back of the building and the Shoal Bay subdivision in front.

Well worn stand, Aramoana.

Grinder, Aramoana

Woolpress, Aramoana. The water press and overhead machines were installed by J. Niven from Napier in 1911

Arlington, Waipukurau

This 13,000 acre property was originally taken up by Captain Alfred Newman of the Indian Navy in 1853. By 1865 it was all freeholded and then leased to William Nelson, who abandoned the lease three years later because of a plague of crickets. In 1878 Newman sold 10,000 acres in 36 sections, including the sections for the proposed township of Wanstead, which never materialised. When he died in 1882, his son Walter took over the remaining 5000 acres. He leased the property to H. S. Cooper, who died in 1899. Newman then sold 3500 acres to Mrs Hooper. She pulled down the 22 roomed homestead built of white pine by Captain Newman and which was riddled with borer and built a new single storeyed homestead in 1902. That same year she also built this woolshed as the previous one was blown down by a gale. After the 1st World War most of the property was divided up for Soldier Settlement. In 1965 John and Richard Mackie, Mrs Hooper's grandsons took over the 500 acre homestead block.

Big Hill

Originally part of the 20,000 acre Kereru Station taken up by J.N.Williams and Colonel Jasper Herrick, the 7000 acres of Big Hill were sold to Owen Monckton in 1905. It was bought back by the sisters Gwen Malden and Ruth Nelson in 1944 when they bought Kereru. After some development they sold it again to the Glazebrook brothers, Garry and Derek, of Washpool Station. It is now owned and run by Bill Glazebrook, Derek's son.

Blackhead shepherd's cottage and Blackhead promontory in the background. Captain Cook named this headland Blackhead in 1769 because it showed up black against the horizon.

Blackhead

This 22,000 block was bought off Pourerere in 1873 by J. H. Coleman and Alexander McHardy, and at that stage was not much more than a steep wilderness covered in fern, titoki and scrub. The Coleman, McHardy partnership, which also had land at Pakowhai near Hastings, dissolved in 1878, when McHardy bought Coleman's share for 71,500 pounds. The station still uses the original brand of C and M. Alexander McHardy, who had been a champion highland dancer back in Scotland, died in 1899 aged 69 after performing the Highland Fling at the Palmerston North Opera House. His two sons carried on developing the property and during the 1900's 30,000 sheep and 3,000 head of cattle were being carried. One year they shore 1500 bales of wool. In 1907 14,000 acres was taken off and called Aramoana for the second Alexander McHardy, with Leslie McHardy taking Blackhead. He was one of the first farmers in Hawkes to install shearing machines, eventually increasing the number from 8 to 24 in this shed. The wool was loaded from drays into surfboats and taken out to coastal ships, weather permitting. In 1961 the remaining 3000 acres of Blackhead was divided between the McHardy brothers, leaving the property at 1500 acres. Sadly the two storeyed homestead with thirty rooms burnt to the ground in 1965. The McHardy's sold Blackhead to John and Marian McFee in 1972.

Bloomfield

Robert Franklin first took up 250 acres of matai, totara and rimu in 1888. He burnt some of the bush and planted rape but couldn't get the stock through the tortuous bush, so the rape flowered into a golden mass in the spring giving the property its name, Bloomfield. The woolshed was built around this time. Franklin was a first class shearer and ran a team of twelve bullocks. The first trip from Ti Tree Point, where they lived, to Dannevirke, a 62 mile trip, took six days. By the time Robert died in 1897 of pneumonia, Bloomfield was 4000 acres. His wife Ellen eventually divided the property between her five sons. She lived in the homestead until 1934 when she was killed in a fire that burnt the building to the ground. Various generations have brought the property back to 1500 acres. Michael Franklin is the fourth generation to farm there, and he has two sons

Burnview

Originally part of the 10,000 acre Pipi Bank property applied for by David Speedy in 1856. Pipi Bank was run by his three sons, John, William and Graham, until they divided the property in three in 1876. John Speedy took Burnview and built this woolshed in 1904. By the time John died in 1914 the station was 7800 acres. The 4300 acre property is now run in trust for his descendants, the Armstrong and Riddell families.

Burnview, Herbertville

Angus Gordon

Cabbage Tree Flat Waimarama

This old shed, built in 1912, has been sidelined by a modern shed on this 5700 acre station, but is still used for dagging and overflows. Douglas Stewart bought this property in 1922 from Mr Stratton. who was the manager for G.P. and Airini Donnelly's Waipuka block at Waimarama. The property was originally called Big Stone Block and comprised 950 acres of freehold and 1300 acres which are still leased from the Taikatai Family. It is now run by Donald's son David (Snow) and Helen, and carries up to 25,000 stock units.

Graffitti, Cape Kidnappers shed

Cape Kidnappers

Kidnappers woolshed from the golf course with the Farm Lodge behind. Wall Street maestro, Julian Robertson with his wife Josie, bought the 5500 acre property in 2002, and then built this world class lodge and golf course. The woolshed, built in 1935, 10 years after the property was bought from Clifton Station, was originally down beside the Maraetotara River, and was dismantled and moved up to its present site in the middle of the farm after the 2nd World War by the then owners, the Neilsons, who called their property Summerlee. The Robertsons changed the name to Cape Kidnappers Station. There is now a 9 kilometre vermin proof fence protecting the whole of the coastal peninsula, where a Sanctuary, for the propogating of endangered N.Z. birdlife, including about 80 kiwis, now thrives.

Old gate post Chesterhope

Chesterhope shearers quarters.

Chesterhope

This original 16 stand blade shearing shed, (and now an 8 stand machine shed,) situated between Pakowhai Road and the Hastings/Napier Expressway was cut up into three parts, the woolroom, and the two shearing boards and moved onto this 1700 acre property by horses from Mangaterere, when David Fernie bought the block in 1908. The farm was completely flat, except for the slight rise where the buildings were built. In 1938, before all the stop banks that are now there were built, a devestating flood came through like a wall of water, killing 6000 sheep. Davis Fernie, who was trying to muster the sheep to the relative safety of the woolshed area, lost all his dogs as his horse swam him to safety. When he died, he left the farm, along with Moeangiangi, to his daughter Joan Fernie, who lived in the house off Pakowhai Road until she died in 2007, aged 90. The Joan Fernie Charitable Trust, which has been supervised by Malcolm MacDonald, also a trustee, for over 50 years, runs all three Fernie blocks, Chesterhope, Moeangiangi and Mangatapiri.

Chestermans', Maraetotara Road

Clifton

Clifton, with red hot pokers in the foreground and Clifton Cafe, built in 1999, in the background. The design for the cafe were based on the original Clifton woolshed built in the 1860's by James Gillespie Gordon, the original pioneer, before the current woolshed was buillt in 1886 by his grandson, Frank Gordon. The new one had 20 blade shearing stands, 10 down each side of the woolroom. 25,000 sheep were shorn a year. It was converted to a 12 stand machine shed in the late 1890's. Clifton, originally 13,500 acres, was subdivided over the years between the three Gordon brothers, with Frank retaining 8000 acres of Clifton, which included Cape Kidnappers. In 1925 he sold 5300 acres of the Cape Block to Colonel Neilson. That property has since changed hands twice and is now owned by an American family, the Robertsons who call their property Cape Kidnappers Station. Clifton, now 2000 acres, is run by Angus and his son Tom Gordon, the sixth generation Gordon on the place. It has diversified into, amongst other thing, hospitaiity, with the cafe and glamping accomodation, squash grown for the Japanese market, red hot pokers for traditional seat weaving, forestry, and sheep shearing shows in the woolshed for the cruise ship visitors, but still winters around 7000 stock units comprising cows and fattening lambs. The original brand of an Anchor over J.G.G. is still in use today.

Ploughing the old way. Antique machinery day at Clifton, 2010.

Clifton with the old stables in the foreground.

Clifton Woolroom and museum.

Blade Shearers outside Clifton woolshed, 1893. Frank Gordon, seated with boater on.

Squash harvest, Clifton.

Tom Gordon, 6th generation at Clifton. Model blade shearer in background. The woolshed is used as a museum and venue for farm and dog shows, mainly for tourists off the cruise ships.

Droxford, near Dannevirke. This area is now all in dairy farms.

Droxford

Edenham

Originally part of a 25,000 acre block applied for by Alfred Chapman and the Rhodes Brothers in 1851, it had 14,000 acres of freehold by the time the partnership was dissolved in 1873. When Chapman died, Joseph Rhodes acquired the homestead block of 8156 acres, which was then sold to J.N.Williams in 1879. He increased the property to 16500 acres. The station was subdivided between members of his family before he died in 1915. Oscar Nilsson bought the 3,375 acres of the homestead block. When he died in 1960 the property was run by his estate until it was sold to Landcorp in the early 2000's.

Fairfield, Onga Onga

H.H. Bridge ought this 7500 acre farm from the original owners, the Fannins, in 1865 and by 1872 he had 7000 sheep on the property. He also cut off 78 sections which became the township of Onga Onga. After a succession of owners and subdivisions the 734 acre property was sold in 1956 to the Wilson brothers, sons of the well known Hawkes Bay historian, J.G.Wilson. After 10 years the partnership was dissolved with J.R.G. Wilson running the property for another 40 years before handing over to his son Greg, who with his wife Liz, has been cropping and fattening bulls on the property since then.

Famous Times | 29

Fairfield Graffiti

Forest Gate, Onga Onga

This 13,000 acre property was farmed in partnership by J. Russell Duncan and his brother-in-law, Colonel Jasper Herrick, who left Kereru Station in 1868 after the death of his first wife and later married Emily, Duncan's sister. Herrick eventually took over Forest Gate in his own right. Herrick was elected to the Hawkes Bay Provincial Council in 1876. A keen botanist, he died precipitously in 1890 when he fell over the Waihi waterfall on his Oporae property near Dannevirke while gathering ferns. In 1901 the Seddon Government compulsorily acquired Forest Gate from his widow under the new Land Acquisition Act for Closer Settlement. There was considerable indignation among the farming community that a widow and six children were being forced to sell. The trustees managed to eventually get a pound per acre more for the land. The 9000 acre property was then subdivided into seventeen farming blocks and seventeen smaller blocks around Onga Onga township. (The sword that was presented to Colonel Herrick by Queen Victoria for his exploits in the war against Te Kooti was presented to the Onga Onga museum by the Herrick family in 1966.) The homestead block of 844 acres was sold to Alexander Mackie, who sold it again in 1934 to Duncan Holden, a leading light in the NZ horse world. The Holden family are now into their third generation of ownership.

Glen Aros

In 1899 the MacFarlane brothers, Willie and James, bought 4000 acres from Maraekakaho Station, where they had been working for their cousin Sir Donald MacLean. They named their property Mount Lookout and ran it in partnership for 12 years before dividing it between them. Willie took Waiteranui and formed a well known Angus stud there, which is still run successfully by his grandson, Will. James took Glen Aros and built this 5 stand woolshed at that time. The 600 hectare farm, is now owned by David Grieve and managed by his son Tim.

Glenross, off the Taihape Road

This was part of the original shed built in the 1880's by J.G.Kinross. The homestead in the background was built in 1879, but is owned separately by David Hildreth, who also owns the Glenross property. The Jim Gunsons own the woolshed and 500 acres and farm it under the Branson Trust.

Gruinard, Mackenzie Road

This 1400 acre property was retained from the sale of Kahuranaki in 1897 for C.F.Mackenzie and his wife, who was W.A.X.Couper's neice. The 6 stand woolshed was built in 1904. It was repiled in the 1990's by the owners at the time, Bruce and Jenny McGregor, who have since sold the property in 2014 to the Hunsberger family.

Supervisor, Gwavas.

1890's, Gwavas.

Part of the water press at Gwavas.

Tristam and Carola Hudson, Gwavas.

Water press, Gwavas.

Gwavas

This 30,000 acre block at Tikokino was originally taken up by C.J. Pharazyn in the early 1850's, but within a short time he was joined by Major George Gwavas Carlyon, who had served in the Crimean War amongst other Imperial adventures. The property was named Gwavas after their Cornish family name. The original homestead that he brought his family to in a bullock wagon, was built from timber milled on the station, and had dormer windows and a shingled roof. It is still lived in by his ancestors, Michael and Carola Hudson. When the Major died in 1875 his son Arthur Spry Carlyon took over part of the property, eventually acquiring the remainder of the property from his family. In 1891 he built the huge 30 room homestead, which is still in use today as a tourist lodge, owned and run by Phyllida (ex Hudson) and her husband Stuart Gibson. A.S.G. laid out the gardens with rare shrubs and trees assisted by his head gardener, John Nichol, who worked on Gwavas for fifty-five years. The Nichols moved into the old homestead when the new one was finished, and Mrs Nichol, who died when she was in her nineties, saw five generations of Carlyons at Gwavas. A.S.G. Carlyon also established one of the first Aberdeen Angus studs in Hawkes Bay and in 1902 bought one of the first cars into Hawkes Bay, a 12 horse power Daimler. They then had to build bridges over the streams to get it out of the station as it had arrived in a packing case. The woolshed, built in the 1880's with 10 stands down both sides, originally had a shingles roof. By 1900 they were shearing 21,000 sheep in it. It had a hydraulic press, which still works today, and the Burgon and Wolesley shearing machines were run by a six horse power Marshall traction engine. By 1912 the Angus stud had grown to 100 cows, there were fifty horses working on the property, there were 25 permanent people employed on the place, rising to about 65 at shearing time, and A.S.G. owned a Rolls Royce and a Cadillac, taking only an hour and a half to make the 27 mile journey to Napier. In 1913 Gwavas was reduced to 15,000 acres, wintering 15,000 ewes and 1000 cattle, and then in 1915, 6000 acres were sold in twelve lots. When A.S.G. died in 1928 the station was left in trust to his son Ernest Tristam Rupert Carlyon and his daughter, Olga Hudson. Captain Rupert Carlyon served in the 1st World war and died during the 2nd World War. Eventually after more disposals of land, the 2900 remaining acres of Gwavas were taken over by the Hudsons, with Michael Hudson, Olga's son, and his wife Carola, running the 2900 acre property for 35 odd years, until their son John took over in the early 90's. He and his wife Fiona sold the property in 2011 to the Te Awa Hohonu Forest Trust, but Michael, Carola and the Gibsons still retain the two old homesteads, the extensive bush area and the beautiful forest garden started by A.S.G. and extended by themselves.

Haupouri, Ocean Beach, looking towards the Whakapau Bluff

Haupouri

This was the outstation at Ocean Beach for Clifton before being subdivided off in 1912 for Edward Gordon. Frank Gordon of Clifton then built this 6 stand shed for his absentee brother using one of the six stand shafts from Clifton. Originally the property was 6000 acres, but part of it was taken off to increase the acreage of Taurapa Station, which was owned by another brother, Charles. Edward's nephew Ian took over the Haupouri block of 3700 acres when Edward died in 1914, with 2200 acres of the farm now being run by his great grand-niece, Hilary Hansen, the seventh generation Gordon. The other 1500 acres is farmed in partnership with Andy Lowe, who also now owns the woolshed block. He and his wife Liz, with help from Warwick and Juliet Hansen, Hilary's parents, and Julian and Josie Robertson of Cape Kidnappers Station, were responsible for creating the Cape Sanctuary by building a 9 kilometre vermin proof fence in 2009 from Ocean Beach to the Clifton cliffs, to protect the whole of the Cape peninsula area.

Herbertville

This was the original shed for Joseph Herbert, who established the township of Wainui, which later became Herbertville, on the beach near Cape Turnagain, to cater to the drovers and travellers moving up and down the coast to the Wairarapa and Wellington.

Well greased floor, Hedgeley

Hedgeley, Eskdale

This shed, once a familiar sight on the drive through the Esk Valley, burnt down in 2011 not long after it was photographed, and has been replaced by a modern shed. This was originally a ten stand blade shearing shed for the station, which reached 10,000 acres by 1905 under the ownership of Thomas Clark.

Pigeon loft, Hedgeley

Hilton, Middle Road

It was built in the 1870's as a 7 stand shed for Robert Mackenzie, who acquired the 1700 acre property as a dowry when he married Janet Couper, the daughter of W.A.X.Couper of Kahuranaki. His great great grandson, Paul Mackenzie, runs the 1200 acre farm.

Hilton- Mackenzies.

Kahuranaki looking across the river to the back of Mt Erin.

Kahuranaki

Built on the banks of the Tuki Tuki River in the late 1870's by W.A.X. Couper whose father had bought and leased the 13000 acre property in 1854. It was an 18 stand blade shearing shed, shearing around 16,000 sheep a year. It was later converted to an 8 stand machine shed. The wool was taken down the river by raft to the mouth of the river and then shipped to Ahuriri. The property was cut up and sold in 1897. The woolshed is no longer in use but is owned by Bill and Denise Dodds, who turned the top storey wool room in a dwelling.

Spring shearing, Kahuranaki Station. Mt Kahuranaki looms over the 2500 acre property now owned by the Greenwood family.

Kelvin Grove.

Kelvin Grove

This property was bought in 1888 by George Crosse, who was previously the Rabbit Board Inspector at Herbertville. He built this shed in 1897 and it was converted to machines in 1907. The 1090 hectares is now farmed by Grant and Hamish Crosse, whose great great grandfather first arrived in New Zealand in 1849.

Poukawa Hills, late summer

Longlands shed, Maraekakaho Road

This was part of a larger woolshed that was built for the 9500 acre Longlands Station leased by J. H. Coleman from the Maoris in 1866. He then sold to Robert Farmer and James Watt in 1873, and it was they who freeholded the property. The seventeen stand woolshed was originally at the Pukahu end of the property. This part was cut off and brought to its present site by Watt's son E. J. Watt, who became well known in Hawkes Bay as a race horse breeder. His stallion, Merriwee, which won the Melbourne Cup in 1889, was buried under one of the gum trees behind the cottage. The Hawkes Bay Expressway now runs directly through where the cottage stood.

Mangatapiri

Built in 1912 when the 6000 acre property was first acquired from St Lawrence Station by Walter Fernie, this magnificent 8 stand shed can nightpen 1200 sheep. When Walter Fernie died he left the property to his nephew Jack Roberts and his neice Joan Fernie, who eventually acquired the whole property. The station is now part of the Joan Fernie Charitable Trust, which also runs Moeangiangi and Chesterhope.

Mangatapiri woolshed and shearers quarters with the Silver Range in the background.

Mangatarata, Waipukurau

This magnificent property was the second run to be taken up in Hawkes Bay. David Gollan, who applied for 17000 acres in 1853, was joined by his brother Kenneth, and by 1858 the brothers owned 30,000 acres. They subdivided the property again in the early 1860's. When David died in 1887 his son Spencer inherited it. He raised some famous racehorses there including the NZ Cup Winner, Tiraillerie, in 1898. His half brother, Louis De Pelichet, managed the station from 1885 and by 1900 was shearing over 40,000 sheep in this shed, which started as a 24 stand blade shearing shed in the 1880's, and was converted to a 12 stand machine shed in the turn of the century. It is now a six stand machine shed, lovingly maintained by its present owners, the Barham family, who farm approximately 10,000 stock units on 2500 acres.

Mangatoro, Dannevirke

Captain George Douglas Hamilton of the 11th Hussars and a veteran of the Maori Wars, originally leased 30,000 acres from the Maori owners, but they kept a strict eye on him, not allowing he and his partner John Wilkinson to touch the bush or take his wool clip down the Manawatu River. The 8 stand woolshed with a shingles roof was built approximately in the 1870's but has been out of use for many years. 5000 acres were eventually freeholded but in 1884 the block was taken over by the Bank of New Zealand. In 1902 the remaining 20,000 acres of leasehold were bought by the Government and cut into 26 sections for ballot under the Lands Settlement Act. In 1908 the Government sold the homestead block to William Knight, despite lengthy court proceedings by Hamilton, who died a broken man in 1911. Knight's son A.B. Knight, who ran the block in conjunction with Tiratu, where he had a sawmill, cut the property up after the 1st World War. The homestead block of 475 acres went to Donald Grant, who established the famous Mangatoro Angus Stud there. His daughter, Maisie Grant took over the stud in 1965 and maintained the high profile. The stud has since been disbanded. The 360 acre farm is now run by Ian Henderson.

Mower blades, Mangatoro.

Mangatoro.

Maraekakaho. The expert's notice. There were 14 Maori shearers down one side of the shed and 14 pakehas on the other side.

Maraekakaho

Built in the 1880's for Donald McLean, the Government Land Commissioner responsible for buying most of the land in Hawkes Bay for the Government from the Maoris in the 1850's. It was one of the largest in the country with 28 stands and was one of the first to have shearing machines. It could carry 5000 sheep in the night pens. Starting out as a 9000 acre station in 1858 the station grew to 50,777 acres in the 1880's under the stewardship of R.D.D. MacLean, Sir Donald's son, who also changed the spelling of the family name. By the 1890's there were 63,000 sheep being shorn in the shed, and a permanent staff of 80, many of them Scots brought over as shepherds. There were also 70 Clydesdale brood mares, and 40 Welsh pony mares, which were famous all over Hawkes Bay. With the introduction of the heavy land tax introduced by the Seddon Government in the 1890's the land began to be subdivided up, culminating in the eventual sale of the remaining property in 1930, after the death of Sir R.D.D.MacLean in 1929. On the original 50,777 acres there were approximately 62 farms in the 1970's.

Maraetotara Road

Matapiro

Originally a 22,500 acre block, it had many owners, until Walter Shrimton bought the property in 1875. He was a leading light in Hawkes Bay for many years being Chairman of the Hawkes Bay County Coucil for 30 years and Chairman of the Hawkes Bay Hospital Board for 25 years. By 1912 the property was 10,000 acres and shearing 16,000 sheep annually. When he died in 1936 the property was further divided up into the present day 4750 acres (1900 hectares) and was managed for many years for the Walter Shrimpton Estate until it was sold in 2004 to Ken Syminton, a major shareholder of Hellabys.

Old shearers' quarters Matapiro.

Matapiro.

Middle Road

A W.A.X Couper property.

Moanaroa

Like Akitio, it is not technically in Hawkes Bay, but gravitates to Weber and Dannevirke, so I have included it. It is also one of the three architecturally designed sheds, along with Tautane and Akitio, in the area. Built in the 1883 for Mairananga Station, it was originally a 16 stand blade shearing shed, with 8 stands down either side. It is the only one of the three that has retained the original stands, using 6 on the southern side. The station was divided in two in 1936 and the shed changed its name to Moanaroa, and was owned by P.B.Smith. The 4000 acre property is now farmed by Dan and Barbara Ramsden. They have kept the woolshed in immaculate condition, and have changed the colour of the roof to grey since this photo was taken.

Moeangiangi, Waikari.

Bringing in the sheep, Moeangiangi.

Moeangiangi

This 9000 acre property near Mohaka had many early owners including James Gillespie Gordon of Clifton, the first owner, and was a difficult property to run because of all the gorges and fern. David Fernie bought it in 1913, built this 8 stand shed and developed it into a magnificent station carrying approximately 30,000 stock units today. 608 bales of wool went out of the shed in 1966. It is still owned by the Fernie Trust.

Moeangiangi's well lit shearing board.

Upstairs, Mokopeka. The winch for getting the bales upstairs for storage.

Mokopeka cobwebs.

Mokopeka. Discarded wool press

Mokopeka. Complimentary colour scheme.

Mokopeka

This 6500 acre block was taken off Te Mata in 1887 by John Chambers for his son, also John, who then built this 16 stand blade shearing shed. John, an enterprising engineering inventor, designed his own electric shearing machines, which he had made in America and then installed in the shed in the early 1900's. He also designed his own electric power station using water from the Maraetotara River, which provided power to the station for 75 years and is still in use today. This was unique at the time as very few people even understood the principles or the potential for electric power. He also designed and built the first electric stove in N.Z. as well as electric heaters and a cool room. In 1959 after various family members had died, Mokopeka Farm Ltd was created by John's nephew, John Mason Chambers. The company bought the homestead and 682 acres for his son John Patrick Chambers and his daughter Mrs Shirley Wood. Unfortunately, Johnny, as he was called, died in a car accident in 1964. The remaining area of Mokopeka was sold in 1965, with Johnny's wife Sandra staying on in the homestead with her three children and farming the 1000 acres in the Company. Johnny's son Richard sold the whole block to a developer in 2007 but continues to lease the farm back.

Okawa.

Blade shearers, Okawa, 1885

Okawa

This shed is now disused having been replaced by a modern shed. The first Thomas Lowry leased 10,577 acres from the chief Tareha Te Moananui in 1852. By 1855 he was able to start freeholding the property. In 1870 his brother-in-law, Nathamiel Beamish, became the manager. By 1876 they were shearing 20,000 sheep in this sixteen stand shed. His son, the second Thomas, returned in 1888, aged 22, from England where he been educated at Cirencester Agricultural College and Cambridge University. He married Helen Watt from Longlands, and like his brother-in-law, E.J.Watt, became a prominent breeder of racehorses, Desert Gold being one of the best. By the early 1900's the station had reached its peak of 20,000 acres, with 35,000 sheep being shorn in this shed, which had been converted to a machine shed using a Wolseley oil engine. T.H. Lowry contributed largely to the war effort in the 1st World War, building the Lowry Hut at Etaples, and his wife was the president of the N.Z. Red Cross, receiving the O.B.E. for her work. In the 2nd World War Lowry built 2 more huts, one in Egypt and one in Italy. These huts were run by the Y.M.C.A. for the soldiers' recreation. When T.H. died in 1944, the remaining property that hadn't been sold was divided between his three sons, Tom, Jim and Ralf. Each received 3000 acres. T.C. Lowry, who gained a Cambridge blue for cricket, took over the homestead block and the horse stud, which became famous throughout the Antipodes. He had the distinction of playing cricket for both the M.C.C. and New Zealand. He captained New Zealand in 1927 and managed the team in 1937. Okawa is now being run by the 5th Tom Lowry.

Olrig

Two properties were bought by H.W.K.Smith in 1859 and 1861 to give him a 28,000 acre property which he named Olrig. When he died in 1876, the land went into trust for his four sons, Hector, Charles, James and Frank. By 1900 there were 30,000 sheep on the station, In 1907 the Government bought 12,000 acres of the best land from James and Frank under the Land Acquisition Act. This became the Mangatahi settlement, which was subdivided into 22 farms and sold. The current woolshed was built in 1907 by Charles and Hector Smith, who divided the station between them into two properties, Olrig and Whanakino, but ran them as a partnership of 15,000 acres until 1922. 27,000 sheep were shorn in this modern twelve stand shed in 1909 producing 437 bales of wool. On the dissolution of the partnership, various blocks of Olrig were sold bringing it down to 4000 acres of well farmed country shearing up to 21000 sheep a year. In 2001 John Milmine bought 2000 acres leaving 2100 still in the original family. It is farmed by Richard Paterson.

Olrig stables and machinery sheds.

Omakere. Sheep on road to Pourerere

Oreka

Graffitti in the Oreka shed so delicately inscribed by young Margot Lowry, daughter of Jamie and Pru Lowry. Oreka, 3700 acres, was part of Okawa and was inherited by J.N.Lowry, son of T.H, and father of Jamie, in 1944. Jamie now farms in partnership with his son Adam, also a fifth generation Lowry.

Oringi

Dancing calves, Oringi. Situated on the banks of the Manawatu River, this pig and wild dog infested 16,000 acre leasehold property was sold by J.D.Ormond in 1875 to Henry Gaisford. By 1879 he had 45,000 acres of leasehold land stretching down both sides of the Manawatu River, with a woolshed on each side. The 560 acre property is now owned by the Arends family, and there are no sheep on the farm.

Orua Wharo, Takapau

In 1851 the Honorable John Johnston, Wellington businessman and politician, walked through Hawkes Bay from Wellington with Alex St Clair Inglis and John Harding, later of Mount Vernon, and applied to lease 9000 acres when he returned to Wellington. It wasn't until 1862 that he was able to buy the land and by 1870 he had 17,726 acres. When he first took up the lease he had granted the grazing rights to Alex St Clair Inglis and Charles Gully, brother of W.C. Gully, who became the Speaker of the British House of Commons. They were also cousins of John Gully, the artist. In 1861 Sydney Johnston, John's son came to Orua Wharo and lived in a bark hut until he took over running the property in 1865. By 1885 the Johnstons were shearing 30,000 sheep in this 16 stand shed. Shearing machines were installed in 1900. Five years after Sydney died in 1917, his daughter, Agnes, married John Rolleston MP, and they had a son Sydney Christopher in 1923. He was born in the Blue Room in the magnificent homestead, which was used as a vice regal residence by Lord Plunket and Lord Jellicoe during the family's absence in England in the early 1920's, and which still stands today. By 1951 the property had been reduced to 2800 acres, and after Sydney Rolleston was killed in a tractor accident in 1953, the property has since been run in trust for his daughter, Caroline Innes.

College Road, Te Aute

Papakihaua, Porangahau

This shed was built in 1908 when the Hunter Brothers divided Porangahau Station in half, with Paul Hunter calling his 16,000 acres by the local name for the area. It is now farmed by Rob Hunter and his family.

Patangata

Built by Alfred Dillon in 1900 for the 2500 acres he had bought off Homewood Station, this smaller five stand shed shore 8000 sheep a year at its peak. Alfred Dillon was a member for Parliament, who campaigned for closer land settlement for the smaller farmers. His spacious homestead became a centre for balls and hospitality in the area with a dance floor being put into the woolshed. The estate was subdivided up after his death in 1915.

Patoka Hill.

Patoka

It began it's identity when T.E.Crosse bought 10,000 acres in 1902, from the original 30,000 first bought by Sir George Whitmore. The woolshed was built in 1898 before the Crosses bought the property and was a 16 stand blade shearing shed for only two years before being converted to machines. It is now an 8 stand shed. The station only ran 13,000 sheep as 4000 acres was still in native fern and scrub. Over the years subdivisions were made until the station settled on it's 3000 acres of very well farmed country today. It is run by the 4th generation of Crosses, Ben and Suzie, who have three children.

Poporangi, Kereru

This property reached its peak in the 1880's and 90's when John Anderson came to manage the 13,000 acre station for the partnership he had formed with William Royse. In 1883, 21,000 sheep were shorn in this shed, producing 259 bales of wool. Anderson was an excellent judge of stock, winning 11 first prizes at the 1886 Hawkes Bay A. & P. Society. The sheep were still all Merinos in 1894, but Lincolns were introduced the next year. Anderson had the Kereru Post Office and library in his homestead and public worship was also carried out there. Poporangi became one of the showplaces of Hawkes Bay, with the Governor General, Lord Glasgow being entertained there in 1896. After Anderson died in 1905 the property went into decline with large parts of the back country reverting to manuka and fern. The family sold 2300 acres to P.R. (Dick) Gaddum in 1950, and it was his success in bringing the property back into full production that persauded the government to buy the rest of the station for Soldier Settlement, putting a further 9 soldiers on farms in the Mangleton area.

Porangahau

This massive shed, originally 28 blade shearing stands, with 16 stands down both sides, was built of kauri milled in Northland. George Hunter applied for the first lease in 1854 and by the 1860's had 32,000 acres which were eventually freeholded. His two brothers, David and William managed the property for him. They drove the first 500 Merino ewes up from Wellington and lived in a primitive shack on the property. By 1875 they were shearing 27,000 sheep a year in this shed. George's two sons, George, later Sir George, and Paul arrived in 1877 to take over the station. Sheep returns reached 51,000 in 1900, when as many as 4000 sheep could be shorn in the shed on a good day. The partnership lasted 28 years until 1908 when the brothers divided the property in half. George, who took Porangahau, was a Member of Parliament for Waipawa for 22 years, and also a member of the Patangata County Council for thirty years, many of them as Chairman. He would ride to and from the meetings in Waipukurau in one day. He was knighted in 1920. By the time he died in 1930 he had gifted 2800 acres for Soldier Settlement, and sold another 9 properties. The 2500 remaining acreages were farmed by his son in law, John Humphreys for many years. The property is now owned and run by Frank Gordon and his son Michael.

Kingsfisher inspecting the graffitti and fire damage in the Porangahau woolshed.

Rangitapu, Omakere

This shed was built in 1907, when 3000 acres was subdivided off Mangakuri Station for George Coldham Williams, Samuel William's nephew. He had been the manager of Mangakuri, and used to take the services each Sunday in the little church. The station is now owned by the James Aitken family.

Raukawa

The original woolshed burned down in the early 1920's and was replaced by this new six stand shed. Originally 15000 acres of freehold and lease land owned by the McDougall brothers and J.G.Kinross, by 1905 it was 5000 acres and owned by the Harding family of Mount Vernon. Robert Harding, the grandson of the early pioneer John Harding, established a well known Romney Marsh stud here. Over the years the farm was reduced to 1471 acres which was managed by the Robert Harding Trust after his death in 1956. It is now owned by Belinda Rokeby Johnson who bought the property in 1973. She has kept the woolshed in mint condition.

Rochford

This property, once part of Kahuranaki, was retained by W.A.X.Couper's daughter, Mrs Guy Rochford, when the main property was sold on 1897.

Sherenden undergoing renovations in 2009.

Sherenden

Once part of the 30,000 acre Tunanui block owned by the Russell Brothers, the Sherenden block of 10,000 acres was taken off and went to W.R.Russell when the Russell brothers dissolved their partnership in 1896. The woolshed was built then. In 1907 the property was sold to John Lethbridge, who then sold most of the land, excluding 1000 acres, to the government for ballot blocks. The farm is now back up to 1900 acres and is owned by Ivan Grieve, in partnership with his daughter Mary and her husband Michael Groome, who farm the property. They have recently finished spray painting the shed which used about 400 litres of paint. The loft was used to store wool for sometimes up to three years until the prices were right.

Kotri, Springhill

The original 6000 acre Springhill property was sold by Alex St Clair Inglis to Joseph Rhodes in 1873 for 7500 pounds. Joseph Rhodes, who had just dissolved his partnership with Alfred Chapman in Edenham, took a very active part in Hawkes Bay politics, and at a meeting held in the Golden Fleece Hotel in Napier on 20th September, 1857, it was he who moved the resolution that eventually separated Hawkes Bay from Wellington, and formed the Hawkes Bay Provincial Council. He was also closely involved with setting up the Hawkes Bay A. & P. Society. He died in 1905 and in 1913 the station was sold to the Government, who subdivided the block into fifteen sections for sale. This woolshed was called Kotri and was built for one of those properties then.

Springvale, Tikokino

Springvale, Tikokino, was originally 200 acres taken up in 1857 by Johnathan Holden, but rose to 10,000 acres by the late 1860's. It is now 1200 hectares and is still farmed by the David Holdens, 5th generation descendants of the original owners.

St Lawrence, Elsthorpe.

St Lawrence looking towards Elsthorpe.

Catching pens, St Lawrence.

St Lawrence, with stables.

St. Lawrence

The property was originally called Te Kopanga, but the name was changed by Sumner Curling in 1885 to St. Lawrence as he had trouble pronouncing the name. His father, Edward Spencer Curling bought 16,500 acres of scrub covered country in 1852, and built the 16 stand blade shearing shed in 1885. The woolbrand of ESC is still used today and is one of the oldest in the country. The station was managed for 33 years by Gordon Saxby, who transformed the country into a first class sheep run. When St. Lawrence was sold in 1901 to Samuel Williams the flock numbered 30,000, and the Saxby sheep were considered the best ever offered at a North Island clearing sale. In 1912 the H. and W. Williams Memorial Trust subdivided off 13500 acres and leased the properties on a Glasgow lease for 21 years. They kept 3000 acres of the homestead block. In 1974 all but one of the leasehold blocks were sold to the leasees by the Trust. The last one was sold in 1997. In 2006 1500 acres of the homestead block was sold to the L.G.R.Bell Trust. They joined it onto their Cheviot block.

Symes' shed Te Aute Road

Tautane

Tautane with Cape Turnagain in the background. In 1902 this 9000 acre coastal property at Cape Turnagain was bought from the owners Roberts and Co by the three Herrick brothers, Frank, Edward and Arthur, sons of Colonel Jasper Herrick previously of Forest Gate. As they were only boys at the time, the trustee of their father's estate, J.N.Williams, advised them to buy. Frank eventually managed the station for the brothers. Arthur was killed in the 1st World War. Frank built a large three storeyed homestead in 1912, and started an Aberdeen Angus bull breeding stud in 1918. After successes at the A and P shows, the stud became one of the leading herds in the country. In 1936 Frank bought a Gypsy Moth at the suggestion of Sir Francis Chicester, the famous pioneer pilot, and they attempted to fly from Australia to England. However the adventure ended when Frank walked into the propellers after they had landed in the dark in Baghdad, and he nearly lost his left arm. His brother, Eddy Herrick became widely known in N.Z. for his deer stalking activities. The first moose ever shot in Fiordland by Eddy, as well as one of his famous Wapiti heads, still adorn the walls of Clifton, which is owned by his grandson, Angus Gordon. Tautane remained in the hands of the Herrick family for 110 years until it was sold to the Ngati Kahungunu Investment Company in 2013. The station is leased to the Taratahi Educational Trust, and is still run as a fully operational farm with over 35000 stock units.

Tautane

Cape Turnagain taken from Akitio looking back towards Pipi Bank, Burnview and Tautane.

Tautane with the newly added nightpens at this end. It can nightpen 2000 sheep.

Tautane shearing tallies.

Tautane, 10 stands. Drying wet wool after shearing.

Te Apiti

Originally 14,500 acres, By 1887 when it was owned and leased by the Beetham brothers from the Wairarapa, it ran 23,00 sheep. This woolshed was built in 1898 after the property was reduced to 6000 acres and owned by the J.H.Williams Trust. It then became 3600 acres when Waipoapoa was subdivided off, although they were still run as one property, until 1925, by Richard Sunderland, who married J.H.William's daughter Norah. The station is now owned by Landcorp.

Te Aratipi

This 2000 acre station in a good rainfall area at the top of the Maraetotara has been in the same family, the Palmers, for 100 years. It is now run by Eddy, the fourth generation, and his wife Ro.

Te Aute

This 4 stand shed was once part of a much larger 16 stand shed that serviced 20,000 acres at its height and shore 30,000 sheep. The station was established by the Rev. Samuel Williams at the same time as he was establishing Te Aute College for Maori boys, and was used to fund the development and running of the College. He was also responsible, with the assistance of his nephew, Allen Williams, the farm manager, for draining Roto-a-Tara lake and converting all the land around Pukehou into fertile farmland. In 1888 he became the Archdeacon of Hawkes Bay. When he died in 1907, the land was subdivided up between family members. A lot of the Maori lease land, which he had developed, was returned to the Maori owners. The 600 acres of the home block is now farmed by Brownrigg Agriculture as part of its huge farming operation in the area.

Te Awa, Highway 50, Autumn Shearing

Te Maire, Wairoa

In 1916 the longtime manager of Kiwi Station, Murdoch Mackay, bought 4000 acres from the owners, the Chambers' brothers of Havelock North. As he didn't have a woolshed on the property, the Chambers gave him one of the shafts from the Kiwi woolshed, which he and his son, Norman, along with timber for the new shed, moved by wagon to its present site on the main road from Wairoa to Napier. When Murdoch died in 1928, the property was divided up between his four sons, with Murdoch Gordon Mackay getting the 1100 acre Te Maire block. The property has since been sold and planted in pine trees. The shed, which hosted, amongst other local parties, the 90th birthday party of Mrs Mary Mackay, Murdoch's widow, and the farewell party for Neal McKinnon going to the 1st World War, is now on a 52 acre deer block owned by Paul Morunga.

Te Manuiri, Omakere

Originally the outstation for Pourerere Station, 6000 acres was taken off for Jack Nairn in 1906, when the three Nairn brothers subdidvided Pourerere between them. Jack built this 8 stand shed then. In 1932, 4000 acres was sold to the Smith Brothers, who later divided the property in half. Doug Smith and his son Andrew now own and run the property.

Te Mata

John Chambers began buying portions of land in 1854 until he had 18,000 acres, including Te Mata Peak and all of the land where Havelock North stands today. He subdivided the property in 1886 into three stations for his sons. John took Mokopeka across the Tuki Tuki River, Mason took Tauroa and Bernard got Te Mata. This large shed with a top storey for storing wool was built before the subdivision and still shore 12000 sheep in 1900 on the 4000 acres farmed by Bernard. This visionary man planted some of the first grape vines in Hawkes Bay in 1892, and like his father who brought the first horse and cart into Hawkes Bay, he brought in the first car, an Oldsmobile, which could reach speeds of 15 miles per hour. In 1919 he sold 2800 acres to William Richmond, the founder of the meat exporters W. Richmond Ltd. Richmond left the land to his daughter, who married Ernest Couper, a descendant of W.A.X.Couper of Kahuranaki. The land, now about 300 acres, is owned by his granddaughter, Mary Hutton with her husband Johnny. A large block of land, including the woolshed is now leased to Pernard Ricard for grapes.

Te Mata.

Te Mata lift for getting bales to the top storey woolroom.

Te Onepu. Swinging bottle meant to deter birds.

Catching pen Te Onepu.

Te Onepu

One of the last areas of Hawkes Bay to be developed from scrub and heavy bush, this 1300 acre property was bought by M.E.Groome and D. Ballantyne in 1880. The woolshed was built in the 1890's and had six stands of Wolesley machines installed. The shed, which belongs to Peter and Robin Gray now, has been partly dismantled.

The Mission Farm, Taradale

This original 9 stand shed with a shingles roof, and with all the stands on two sides of the building, was built in the late 1800's by the Catholic Mission, which still owns the property. It is situated on the edge of Taradale and beside the famous winery and Mission Concert grounds. It is still used by the farm which is currently leased to Chris Skerman.

Tourere Woolshed

Typical old sliding door on Tourere woolshed. In 1916 the Chambers brothers of Te Mata, who had bought 5800 acres of Tourere, appointed S.A. Robinson, a very progressive farmer, as the manager. He built the original large woolshed and other buidings at this time. In 1919 the property was divided into nine sections and sold at auction. John Swinburn bought the homestead block, plus two other blocks, bringing the property to 2000 acres. In 1923 he married Mason Chamber's daughter, Helen. Swinburn was also a very progressive farmer, being one of the first to apply superphosphate in the area, and to install electricity. He also developed rotational grazing techniques which were followed closely by Massey College. He also planted many radiata and eucalypt plantations, as well as developing a sophisticated water system. Unfortunately in 1928, his 8 year old daughter, Helen, who was looking after a sheep dog bitch and her puppies in the hay stored in a lean- to against the woolshed, decided the animals needed warming up on a cold day. She and her brother started a fire in the hay which burnt the shed to the ground. But all the puppies and the mother were saved. This door was saved from the old shed. John Swinburn's grandson, Peter, now runs 5000 odd acres from here, having increased the property from 1200 acres.

Tuki Tuki

New electric engine onto the old shaft. This property has been in the Coop family for three generations and is now farmed by Kip and Phillip Coop.

Tunanui

John Russell, now deceased father of the present owners, standing in front of the beautifully maintained woolshed in 2008. He was a grandson of General Russell, who commanded the ANZAC withdrawal from Gallipoli, then commanded the NZ Division in France for the duration of the 1st World War, and was Inspector General of the NZ Forces during the Second World War. Built in 1878 for the Russell brothers, Hamilton and William, it was a 20 stand blade shearing shed for a property that started out at 30,000 acres, but was reduced to 19000 acres in 1874, and then to 9000 acres in 1896, when William took the 10,000 acre Sherenden block. The station, now 2500 acres, with another 1000 acres up the road, and carrying 13000 stock units, is run again by two brothers, Andrew and Sam Russell, the fifth generation on Tunanui. The five stand machine shed is in immaculate order, and is also used as the hospitality area for the 22 pheasant shoots that Andrew and his partners run commercially every year. Andrew is also a founding director of StockX, a stock trading firm.

Tunanui 2008.

Tunanui.

From the Burma Hill looking towards Mt Kahuranaki in the distance

Turiroa, Wairoa

This 3263 acre property, covered with fine stands of matai and kahikatea, was taken up by John and Joseph Powdrell in the 1860's. When John Powdrell's family home was burnt to the ground by Hau Hau rebels, he sold his share to Joseph and went to Taranaki. Joseph then set about stump ploughing and sowing the extensive flat land, after the trees had been milled on their sawmill. The woolshed was built using their own timber. His grandson, Walter Powdrell inherited 1100 acres in 1944 and immediately established the well known Turiroa Angus Stud, which is still run successfully by his son, Rick and his family.

Turiroa old cottage.

Waikaraka, Porangahau

This property was sold to Brian Cocker by the McHardies and is now owned by Kevin Stoddard. It is sadly one of the few examples left of an old shed being retained after a new one has been built.

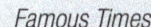

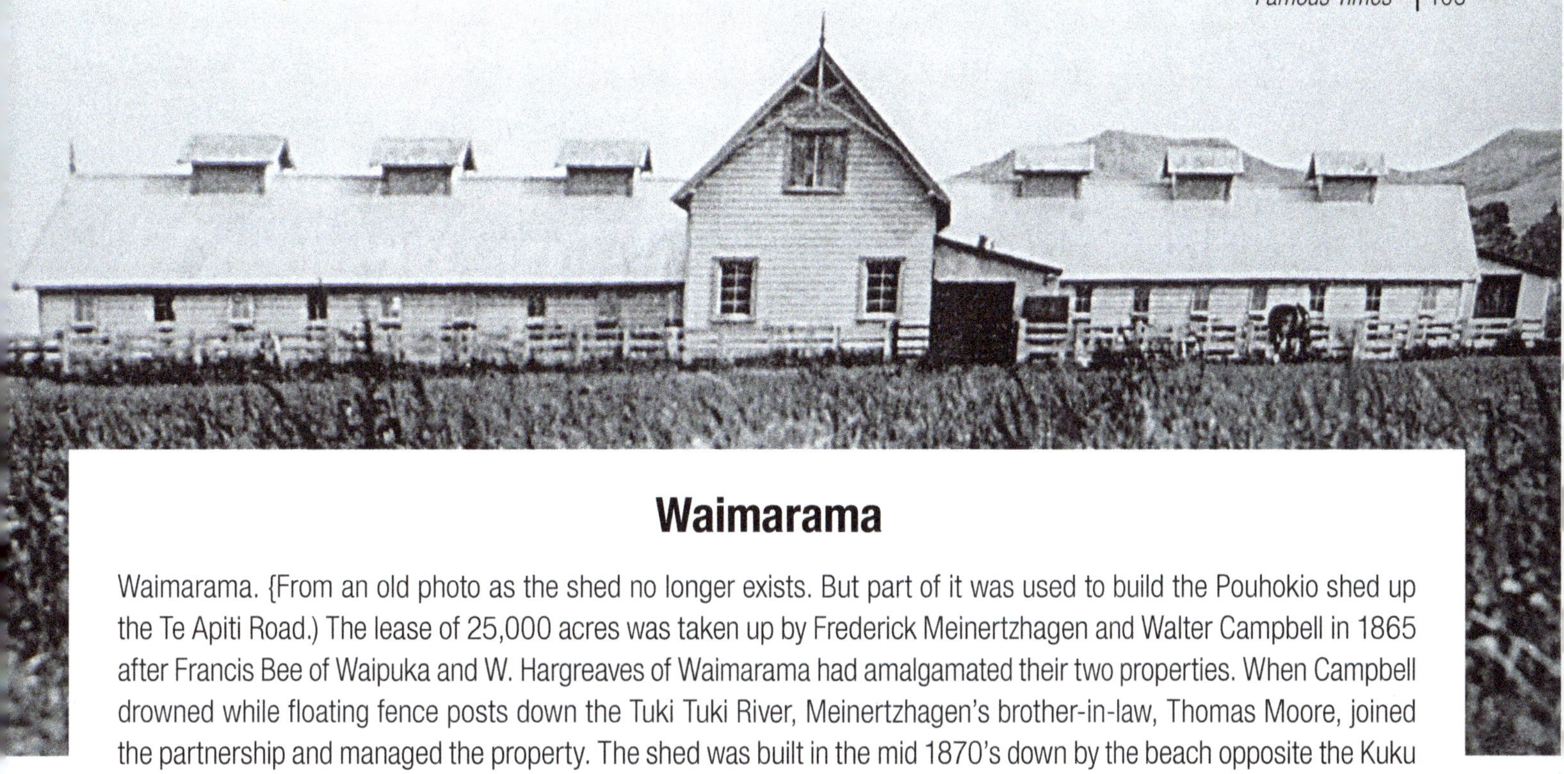

Waimarama

Waimarama. {From an old photo as the shed no longer exists. But part of it was used to build the Pouhokio shed up the Te Apiti Road.) The lease of 25,000 acres was taken up by Frederick Meinertzhagen and Walter Campbell in 1865 after Francis Bee of Waipuka and W. Hargreaves of Waimarama had amalgamated their two properties. When Campbell drowned while floating fence posts down the Tuki Tuki River, Meinertzhagen's brother-in-law, Thomas Moore, joined the partnership and managed the property. The shed was built in the mid 1870's down by the beach opposite the Kuku rocks, which acted as a semi breakwater at low tide for the loading of the wool out to the waiting ships. At its peak in 1900 about 29000 sheep were shorn in the shed. Gertrude Meinertzhagen, Frederick's daughter came back and ran the property for many years, but as the leases expired, 17000 acres of the land reverted to Princess Airini Donnelly, who ran her own station called Waipuka. She and her husband, G.P.Donnelly, had a fraught relationship with their neighbour Gertrude, who was a colourful personality.

Pouhokio, Waimarama. Built from remains of the old Waimarama shed. This is now the woolshed for the Gillies Estate of approx 1500 acres, which is managed by Ken McNeur.

Waipari with a modern woolpress.

Waipari counting out pens.

Waipari

This shed was the original 16 stand blade shearing shed built for Mangakuri Station in approximately 1883. In 1876 Colonel A.H.Russell sold the 21,000 freehold acres with 18,000 sheep for 50,750 pounds to J.N.Williams, who then passed the property onto his cousin Archdeacon Samuel Williams of Te Aute. He built a church on the property and gave all the men a half holiday a week to attend. Those who failed to attend lost their half holiday. By 1900 there were 30,000 sheep on the property. When the Archdeacon died in 1907, the station was divided up between his family. The Waipari block of 5500 acres went to his daughter, Mrs Lucy Warren. Her great great grandson, Mark Warren, still runs 3250 acres of the original property.

Waipari.

Waitukai

Tim and Lucy Gilbertson's colourful shed at Patangata. Tim Gilbertson, poet and at times 'tongue in cheek' rural commentator, is the grandson of J.A.F.Swinburn of Tourere. He was the Mayor of Central Hawkes Bay for 6 years, and was a member on the Hawkes Bay Regional Council for two terms.

Waiwhare, Taihape Road

The 14 stand woolshed was built in 1907 when Waiwhare was subdivided off the vast 68,000 Mangawhare Station which ran right up to the Kaweka Range. It is now owned by David and Linda Ward.

Waiwhare

Wallingford wool room with the old hand wool press.

Wallingford

The first 4000 acres of rolling hills and river flats was selected by the 19 year old John Davies Ormond in 1851 when he accompanied Donald McLean on his first trip to Hawkes Bay. By 1860 the property had grown to 13,400 acres. J.D. Ormond didn't live there for long periods as he was actively involved in National politics, first in Auckland and then in Wellington. His son, also J.D. but known as Jack, and also very active in local politics, took over the station in 1895 when it had reached its peak of 34,000 acres. By 1900 the Ormond flocks were standing at 40,000 sheep. From 1913 on the property began to be subdivided until by 1918 it was 8000 acres. In 1935 the land was cut up into five separate farms for some of the 12 Ormond children, with the homestead block of 1500 acres going to the third J.D. Ormond, who as Chairman of the Meat Producers Board was knighted for his services in 1964. The property is now held in trust for the fifth generation of Ormond children.

Whana Whana

This was the second shed build for the original Whana Whana property in 1898. It was a sixteen stand blade shearing shed which was then converted to a 12 stand machine shed. The property, originally 18,893 acres and running 23,000 sheep, was first bought and leased by Nathaniel Beamish in 1886 and was run by his son George Richard Beamish. It was reduced to 10,245 acres in 1906, and then subdivided between G.R.Beamish's three sons in 1912. Harold took the Whana block, Noel the Awapai block and Eric the Kohatanui block with the woolshed. For many years they all still used this one shed. Bill Beamish, the fifth generation Beamish at Whana Whana, bought the remaining 1800 acres of Kohatanui off Chris Beamish in 2014 and farms it as part of Whana Whana. He and his family live in the second homestead, which was built in 1900, after the original one down by the Ngararoro river was badly flooded. Bill and Penny's son Louis is the sixth generation Beamish on the property, which is now 3750 acres. Of the original 10,000 acres, 8500 acres are still in the Beamish family, with Simon and Josie Beamish running 4500 acres at Awapai, having also bought 2000 acres back off Anthony Beamish.

Whana Whana. Inside the cage is an old Capstan winch connected to the rope above the wool press. It was used to lift the bales up to the mezzanine floor above where about 60 bales could be stored.

Whana Whana. The smoko bell.

Woodbank, Wimbledon

Originally part of Pipi Bank this 3000 property went to Graham Speedy when the property was subdivided by the three brothers in 1876. In 1947 the estate was divided into 5 farms, with Gavin Speedy, Graham's great grandson taking the 600 acre homestead block. Woodbank was the venue for many years of the famous Wimbledon Ewe Fair, with properties like Tautane, Burnview, Pipi Bank and Akitio selling their old ewes here. Peter Williams painted a very fine picture of the sale, which Angus Gordon now has at Clifton.

Also from this Author

IN THE shadow OF THE cape

A history of the Gordon family of Clifton

by Angus Gordon

www.ingramcontent.com/pod-product-compliance
Lightning Source LLC
Chambersburg PA
CBHW061127070526
44584CB00033B/4244